Narad

The Challenge

The Challenge
Copyright : Prisma, Auroville
Author : Narad

First edition 2023

ISBN 978-93-95460-88-0 (Paperpack)
ISBN 978-93-95460-79-8 (ebook)

BISAC Code:
POE000000, POETRY / General
POE009000, POETRY / Asian / General
POE003000, POETRY / Subjects & Themes / Inspirational & Religious

Thema Subject Category:
DC, Poetry
DCF, Poetry by individual poets
D, Biography, Literature and Literary studies
DSC, Literary studies: poetry and poets

Cataloging-in-Publication Data for this title is available from the Library of Congress.

Published by:
PRISMA, an imprint of Digital Media Initiatives
PRISMA, Aurelec/ Prayogshala,
Auroville 605101, Tamil Nadu, India
www.prisma.haus

PREFACE

As one takes up the path of the Integral Yoga a realization comes that there is not a specific path as in all other yogas, especially Raja Yoga, because each has his or her own path to follow according to the guidance given by Sri Aurobindo and the Mother.

This is not an easy yoga for many, when one considers the scale that must be attained, the climb, often arduous challenging and requiring a hard slogging discipline. Yet there is a sunlit path and even though one must go through numerous trials the constant guidance, personal help, grace and blessings of the dual Avatars makes the way much easier.

These poems are about the challenges we face and the Divine Force accompanying us on our path.

We live today in a world that seems beyond our understanding, filled with hate and evil, mistrust and the power grabbing dark forces that are attempting to control humanity under the banner of evil. To many it seems a very dark period and no possibility of overcoming the power of those who have decided to unite with falsehood.

Yet some have seen or felt a light come down upon the earth through a Divine Force termed the Supramental by Sri Aurobindo and the Mother. It promises an end to the reign of these beings of the darkness through the power of a Divine Love that will conquer even death and establish a Divine Life on earth bringing a Light that no minions of the evil forces can abide.

These poems have come down to me during this trying period of the soul. They speak as clearly as possible of the attempts of these demonic elements to wrest from the earth the light and beauty that all cherish. As always, I do not take full credit for what I write, and perhaps it is not often that I receive from the highest sources above the mind, yet I do, however, as always, take credit for my lapses in hearing or the attempts of the mind to think it has the power to improve upon what is coming down!

Hopefully a few of these poems may resound in those who truly aspire for change and know too that change can only come first from within.

Narad

DEDICATION

As always I dedicate these poems to my gurus, Sri Aurobindo and the Mother, who have blessed me in uncounted ways, bearing with all my difficulties and sustaining me in my efforts.

I also dedicate these poems to Nolini Kanta Gupta and Arabinda Basu, the guides who brought me closer to Mother and taught me over many years things that are beyond the mind's knowledge.

Contents

1. Earth and Man — 9
2. A Presence Growing in the Soul — 10
3. Descent into Darkness — 11
4. Do Not the Light Forsake — 12
5. A Force Come Down — 13
6. A Force Divine — 14
7. New Year's Morning A New Year Dawns — 15
8. A Razor's Edge — 16
9. A Visible Unity — 17
10. Anger — 18
11. Auroville, Beloved "Remembrance" — 19
12. Beings of an Alien Kind
    How easily we slip into a state — 22
13. Change — 23
14. Collective Meeting at Unity Pavilion — 24
15. Creating Heaven — 26
16. Endless Strife — 27
17. Fear — 28
18. Golden — 29
19. Momentary Illuminations — 30
20. Our Mortal Fate — 31
21. Sages from Eternity — 32
22. Scorning Truth — 33
23. Take Care — 34
24. The Child — 35
25. The Debate — 36

26. The Enormous Task	37
27. The Hour of God	38
28. The Hour of God is Now	39
29. The light We Seek	40
30. The Nameless Ray	41
31. The Pioneers	42
32. The Reign of Evil Ends	43
33. The Secret of Love	44
34. The Spirit's Home	45
35. The Unfading Ray	46
36. The Warring Tribes	47
37. The Work of Transformation	48
38. The World is Suffering	49
39. The World Made New	50
40. The World Remake	51
41. This World Must Change	52
42. Thy Children Call	53
43. To Conquer Evil's Night	54
44. Truth and Unity	55
45. Truth its Way Will Find	56
46. Truth the Justicer	57
47. Turning of an Age	58
48. Upon the Earth	59
49. We Have Had Enough	60
50. We Try	61
51. What We Need Most	62
52. When Illness Comes	63

Earth and Man

How many borders must we cross to reach
Beyond the limited purview of the mind,
How many books to read that only preach
A liberation of the soul from humankind?

Is this earth not beautiful and pure
And no illusion to that soul of love
Who with steadfast heart the season's deep allure
Sees as divine, a blessing from above.

Why came we here if not to cherish her,
The Mother, Gaia, of the fruitful tree
Her seas, her shores, the beneficent offerer
Divine in essence, consciousness and free.

A Presence Growing in the Soul

One entered into darkness once again
And felt a pressure build within the heart
And as with all transgressions suffered pain
And must make amends or from this world depart.

There is no sin but there is ignorance
Or willful turning back from the light's ray,
Yet there is no fate or sign of random chance
For all here is delight and all is He.

And yet we stumble and we often fall
Though we are not evil as religion says
And deaf to the beauty of the call
Or the descent of the transforming rays.

Although we seem at times far from the goal
There is a Presence growing in the soul.

Descent into Darkness

Tremble the failing legions of darkness now
As Light comes down and the Force of God
Descended on earth in man His Presence to show
The evolution from this earthly sod.

How many aeons past has life appealed
For beauty to unmask its lovely face
And yet the hardness in man will not yield
To the advent of transforming grace.

How many centuries still to come
As man in bitterness battles for a hollow crown
To conquer earth make it his specious home
Descending in darkness down and further down.

Do Not the Light Forsake

Are we indeed cyphers of no value
Is there nothing in the human soul of worth
Nothing that is lasting, nothing true
In mortal beings evident since birth?

The avatars speak of an inner resident
Screened behind the chest, behind the heart
A being growing though divine intent
In the realm of Nature's complicated art.

Will it break through the veils that cover it,
Display through goodness and the holy fire
Or will sleeping man carry it to the pit
Inconscient through the years of his desire?

May it be we shall in mortal years awake
Not linger in tamas * and the Light forsake.

*tamas = inertia, sloth

A Force Come Down

There is a force come down on earth to save
The seeker and the wastrel and the knave
Descending in waves its strength has quickly grown,
A plenitude of Grace from the Unknown
The roads of fixed divinity to pave,
The seeds divine in human hearts has sown.
No longer man need hurry to the grave
For the dual avatars their lives they gave
And all the darker beings now have flown.

December 26, 2021

A Force Divine

If we look with eyes of ignorance
We see the world of ideologies
Gone wild and the anathema of change
Leaves us awash in waves of pounding seas.

Unable to right the rudder of the ship,
Fighting against innumerable foes
Honesty and truthfulness given the slip
And wanton idolatry the insolent pose

Of politics and media whose lies
Told long enough appear to the masses as real,
Dishonesty takes no one by surprise
For many it has a singular appeal.

But working behind the falsehood at its core,
Is a Force Divine who has conquered it before.

January 22, 2022

New Year's Morning
A New Year Dawns

A New Year dawns with the promise of progress
An end of mental argument and forceful wills
Relief of hostile motives and the stress
Of ego natures that their violence fills.

The corridors and vestibules of life
Through which we pass upon our destined way
Facing danger equally and strife,
Evolving soul into a brighter day.

"Enough" the watchman said who sees all things
Unmoved by violence, untouched by sin
It is the psychic being that in us sings
Urging the needed cleansing rite to begin.

The road is daunting but the fearless go
Above the fray to the place that we all know.

January 1, 2022

A Razor's Edge

It is a razor's edge we walk upon
For now the world has grown to satiate
The few who love the darkness, light has gone,
Truth into falsehood grown and love to hate.

The Supermind is felt by more than the few
Who call themselves disciples and devotees,
Yet when the old is dying out the new
Seems distant and falsehood flourishes to please

Those who gravitate towards filth and mire.
Few are they who heed the inner call,
Few who can withstand the cleansing fire
Many know but willingly forestall

Within the truth that has descended here
Perhaps from loneliness, desire or fear.

January 19, 2022

A Visible Unity

Standing on the shoulders of the few
Who reached the realms far above the mind
Gathering in the wisdom of the new
Consciousness so difficult to find

When mind deeply entrenched in duality
Cannot see beyond its clouded wall
The advancing steps of the Deity
Embracing equally the One in all.

A day will come with swiftness to declare
An end to hypocrisy and evil's role
A morn more beautiful arriving where
The wisdom of the wise embrace the fool,

The atheist, the questioner and more.
And souls transformed shall walk through the door
Of light, the golden door of divinity
This earth become a visible unity.

January 28, 2022

Anger

I know the anger that is plaguing you,
Its blinding force entering in waves
Seeming to be yours and yet not true
For it finds reception in the soul that caves
And opens to its debilitating force.
It was in me for years and took control
And still it has not run its final course
Inhibiting the progress of my soul.
At times when I was in a lower state
Of consciousness erupting through my voice
Spewing unpleasantness bordering on hate
I could not cease it having had no choice
Until I stilled the vital in its place
And found in myself the silent home of Grace.

Auroville, Beloved "Remembrance"

Those who departed the fields of Auroville
And scattered on the winds of a turning earth,
Who came at the call of a higher Force and Will
Attending the dream of a sacred city's birth
Are strangers now, their citizenship denied,
The internal passport with its Divine impress
Marked cancelled by the governing elite,
Expired and revoked, the past descried
As momentary phenomena, a stress
Of ephemeral value lost in forgotten years.
Those who knowing knelt before Her feet,
Souls who answered the Divine behest,
Bodies forged in a blaze of burning land -
Names we shall ever remember, ranks of the blest,
By Her presence on earth, touch of
                                    Her transforming hand,
Grace beyond description, transmuting our tears -
Are visitors now in their home of canopied trees
Who seek the truth mid the commerce and interplay
Of mechanic attitudes and anomalies,
A collective of disparate dreams, hopes gone astray
Return to invoke Her name, to consecrate,

Renew the idyll upon this conscious soil
Upholding the charge to build a diviner state,
In this thrice-blessed land resume their Godward toil.

O look to the children whose light-filled forms display
The godhead's sanction, house the resplendent Ray.

(Written towards the end of our stay in the Ashram and earlier in Auroville, at the beginning of the new millennium. Although the poem came as a stream beginning with the first line and ending with the last, it was preceded by certain experiences. Among these was the closing of Auroville to newcomers by the 'Entry Group', being informed of the 'Grace Period' of 5 years for Aurovilians who have left Auroville, after which they are no longer considered 'Aurovilians', the rampant commercialization in Auroville, the planned destruction of dozens, perhaps hundreds of rare trees now 20-30 years old (which were planted in an area designated as the 'outer gardens') to build a lake; countered by the return of some of the first Aurovilians, their heroic work of past years, the love and joy of many Aurovilians, their quiet faith and devoted labour and the light in the eyes of the children.)

Beings of an Alien Kind
How easily we slip into a state

Of apathy or even dare descend
Into the depths of desire to await
The finality that signals journey's end
To this life's growth incommensurate and weak.
What is truly needed is the will
To overcome the false and beauty seek
That all our being here on earth might fill
The nescient void in which our souls have grown.
We speak of human unity but find
That every seeker feels himself alone,
Almost beings of an alien kind.

February 12, 2022

Change

How can we suffer change when all are "right"
And none for others care enough to speak
Of oneness and the great collective dream
Embodying the truth of all mankind.
The ego must break down and the too-sure mind
That "knows" and yet divides in ignorance.
We face the future with unknowing hearts
And our eyes are blinded by the dark desires
Hidden deep within the core of man.
Will there come a healing time on earth
When nations can unite and seek as one
The Truth that leans down from the heights above
The guidance of the Lord enfolding all
Or will we perish in the enduring storm
Of anger and dispute that swallows all
And like the dinosaur that once was king
Give way to the dawning of a higher race
With love and power their mighty force and field.

Collective Meeting at Unity Pavilion

Half awake in the early morn
I heard the OM resound in me
The afternoon and eve were torn
By violent intensity.

I sat and listened two hours and more
As vehement voices from the crown
Shouted to speakers on the floor
And swiftly brought dark forces down.

I did not stay the painful voices
In the maelstrom of the crowd
Shouting forth their obscene choices
Drowning the harmony with loud

Irreverent uncaring shouts
To those desiring calm and peace
Yet in between these vulgar bouts
A few in silence sought release

From enmity and anger's strains
Amongst the turbulent and gross
Looking forward to future gains
Beyond the day's apparent loss.

Will we see Auroville progress
When harmony cannot be found
Will we inversely become less
Fighting to hold the ignorant ground.

Will crashing circumstance descend
Or will love heal and hatred end?

December 20, 2021

Creating Heaven

They say I carry within a deepened peace.
Of this I do not know for worldly things
Upon the spirit come and do not cease,
The constant tribulations and the stings
Of human ego's status seem to increase,
Concerned with all the troubles of the world
And all the vile invectives that are hurled
By those who have no interest in peace.
Nothing can slow the Supramental Force
At work in every soul and every cell,
It will in its own time take its course
Creating heaven from our man-made hell.

Endless Strife

Embedded in falsehood earth is broken again
Or so it seems when surrounding us is pain
And the seeming inevitability of war.
Why can we not rise faultlessly and soar
Above the ego and its archaic rule
As humanity's millions play the fool
Deceived by media and human greed ,
The fodder of lies on which we willingly feed
And live our days in ignorant cocoons
Preferring darkness to the coming noons
And the pleasing of desires to fill a need
For friendship or the producing of a seed
Upon a globe that thrives in endless strife.
For this we came, is this our vaunted life?

March 6, 2022

Fear

There is in some a deep inherent fear
Of Covid and viral fever attacking all,
But fear engenders greater fear and then
Effectually a consciousness lockdown.
The institutions and the governments
Assist the pharmaceuticals who ply
Their wares untested and in massive waves
On children and the elderly, inject
Without discretion or a guiding light.
Perhaps the damage is greater than the cure!
Fear replaces trust and inherent truth,
Towns and cities close their entry gates
And all is in adherence to the law
Imposed on all by the powerful yet blind.

January 28, 2022

Golden

A formless spirit organizing time
Approaches me as from a golden fane,
I write His words as they come down to me
Knowing I am nothing but a scribe.
I impress upon the mind a silence vast,
Unmovable in the daily drama of life
When unimportant seems the world's approach
To finance and the varied governments
Suppressing freedom locking the masses down
A deep-state ideology to rule
And conquer all the souls who disagree.
But I have met Him in the subtle worlds
And with my forehead touched Her sacred feet
And know there is a plan divine at work
Behind the ineffective mind of man
And all one day will see the world anew,
Golden in the beauty of Her Smile.

January 8, 2022

Momentary Illuminations

Momentary illuminations come
But quickly recede behind a veil
Yet the experience can be for some
The Light of Truth that cannot fail.

The artist and the genius both receive
Visions of enlightenment
Allowing them a momentary reprieve
From the loud world's argument.

Is it possible that humanity outgrow
Its karma and need for violence
And find the path of peace on which to go
Recovering the innocence

Of childhood and uncompromising trust
Or will this world turn to dust?

February 7, 2022

Our Mortal Fate

In this maelstrom of opposing ideas,
When harmony is nowhere to be found
And the media exacerbates our fears
Where then for humanity is common ground?

If we could seek collectively a truth
Exemplified by the dual Avatars
And all these vital disturbances soothe
We might then heal the suppurating scars

And the falsehood that encumbers our rise
From ignorance to the Light within that dwells
In our inviolate center and the soul surprise
These forces and annihilate the hells

That evil powers seek to generate,
That we may swiftly change our mortal fate.

January 9, 2022

Sages from Eternity

These souls I meet, unique in strangest ways,
Some certain that they know the destined path,
A few who tread the road that Tantra plays
Yet others seeking the Divine through wrath

And angst at the condition of the human mass,
Seeing the corruption worsening,
Of falsehood's dictates and the sly and crass
Distortions tainting every living thing.

Will crashing circumstances be our fate,
Will evil engulf the world, hypocrisy fill
The human heart and the force of hate
Grow prevalent beyond the human will

For peace and truth and love, the destiny
Foretold by sages from eternity.

January 19, 2022

Scorning Truth

A coconut sells for thirty-three cents
A garland of flowers for a dollar or so
We live our lives in emoluments
As on our shuffling way we go.

We waste in thought our energies
Calculating how much to spend
Forgetting human synergies
And oft we come to a sad end.

Our children dance among the days
In merriment or solitude
Ever worse, for in a daze
They inhale drugs in the interlude.

Between the enticing night and morn
The path to light and Truth they scorn.

January 2, 2022

Take Care

Take care when walking along the precipice
Of falsehood, doubt and life's uncertainty
And the actions of the few who wield their power
To subdue the masses destroying unity
And evil set upon the throne of death.
Lay not thy faith in the seductive word
Or promises without a grain of truth.
Let your voice in the crowd be heard
Amidst the vain of soul and the uncouth
Who stand above you in their fine attire
Seeking ultimate control of men
Whose aspiration is to stoke the fire
Of dissent and cast the world down again.

The Child

This child has wept a thousand, thousand tears
For perfidy of a sacred unity,
Dwelt in her soul the dark unnumbered fears
And the lust that claims each human entity.

Will there ever come solution to it all
Can the indwelling soul arise and say
"I shall walk straight again, I will not fall",
Forego the night, in silence greet the day.

Perhaps it is too early for this child
To renounce the enthralling pleasures of the flesh
And needs more time and years to still be wild
But be aware there is a subtle mesh

That traps the soul in dens of iniquity
We shall pray for her that in time she may be free.

The Debate

I am reading once again of the Hees debacle
And find the falsehood in the book and man
A glaring attempt at personal spectacle
And the support of a consciously evil clan

To pervert by subtle means the Avatar's word.
An inauthentic attempt at diatribe
Written to convince the unknowing herd
And with pervasive words attempt to bribe

Discrediting the Lord with perversion and guile
While to the Trustees managing deceit
Perhaps in a mock literary style
That from Sri Aurobindo we retreat

Accepting falsehood and this person's trust.
Awake disciples reject his book we must.

January 21, 2022

The Enormous Task

The daily news is treachery
And filled with conscious lies
A world of knowing duplicity
In an old familiar guise.

Newspapers too the false exclaim
Intending to deceive
Appropriate error to a name
Without a moment's reprieve.

Where has Truth gone from human eyes
As falsehood daily nears
It is a consciousness to despise
Not to excite fears.

When will it end, the faithful ask
Confronting the enormous task.

January 2, 2022

The Hour of God

The bamboo sings its fluted song
And with it I am carried along,
Among the chattering birds I go
To work in the fields of praise and slow
My breathing and set my mind to rest.
For here in Auroville the test
Is whether these souls can unite
Above the ego and find God-sight
Annulling anger and ill-will
To allow the spirit to rise and fill
These sacred bodies with delight
Emerging from the grip of Night
To greet with reverence the sun,
The Hour of God at last begun.

March 3, 2022

The Hour of God is Now

No angels from the skies can heal our pain
For we who labour here are ignorant
And live within the falsehoods of the hour.
The only possible change is change within
No 'ism' has the power to deny
The enemy that knocks upon our doors.
It is not alone the fearing change in us
But the collective harmony, the earth
In fear beseeches us to heal her wounds.
How many centuries mankind has seen
Depart while he the animal still walks
And speaks with tongue divided to the mass.
A blind humanity unwilling to grow
Into the destined image of the Lord.
The hour of God is now, let all awake.

January 1, 2022

The light We Seek

Peaceful now I am recovering
From debilitating illness and decline
Of temporary health and the painful sting
Of days that are the clear and tortuous sign

That one has not the strength to overcome
The lower forces when they choose to attack,
Though one must pray and occasionally hum
The sacred OM that keeps their entry back

Limiting the damage they inflict
Upon the progress of the consciousness.
The path is long and we build brick by brick
The edifice of soul in our duress

That fallen we may rise again and see
The light we seek in our infirmity.

January 19, 2022

The Nameless Ray

To the precipice and back
We walk our measured blinded way
Looking neither left nor right
Or upwards to receive the day.
The world is filled with violence
And we impotent turn away
Or in the hour faith demands
Kneel and in the moment, pray.
Are we then marionettes on strings
Puppets pulled to our dismay
Flirting with evil or fleeting good
Acting out an unscripted play?

All is an arcane mystery,
There seems no truth that we can say
With certainty, 'This is the truth';
Desire and greed lead us astray

And the sameness of unending hours.
Our lives, our dreams are but Time's prey
Unless we turn to that within,
The light of lights, the nameless Ray.

The Pioneers

We bear the karma of ten thousand lives
And difficulties that we thought were done
Return again and the vital nature thrives
A moment in time when we have lost the One,
Or so it seems in this atmosphere where none
Seems sure of the current path of Auroville,
The wide divergence of the ego's rule
Appears to outward view the world to fill
With argument and hostility, the tool
Of evil forces employing their ill-will.
How soon will peace become our guiding light?
Against all odds Auroville must prevail
And hold the future in our inner sight
We must not be bound again to fall and fail.
The answer lies in Mother's word to all
The Pioneers for they have heard Her call.

March 2, 2022

The Reign of Evil Ends

Now the darkness fast descends,
On earth the broken bodies lie
Terrorism takes its toll
Beneath an ever-watchful eye
That sees and knows and sanctions all
Till evil from our hearts is gone
And lifted is death's sombre pall,
The Light of Truth on earth is won
And the reign of evil ends.

The Secret of Love

Is gratitude sufficient to advance
Along the path so straight yet serpentine
To those unable to discard all and chance
Upon the Way seeking for a sign

Of progress in the challenge of our days.
The sunlit path is there for those who dare
With fortitude and faith, the blinding ways,
The vital's inordinate desire for its fare

Of dark experience and shunning of the light,
Or set our path in the brambles of the mind?
We must keep the Guidance glowing firm and bright
That one day freed of ego we may find

The secret of love that ever informs our days
And live our lives in humility and praise.

January 19, 2022

The Spirit's Home

The City of Dawn is lacking peace
Quarrels and intransigence abide.
Where now the vision of Her Truth, Her Way,
How can we in hostility decide
Her course, the movement she will make
When all can quote Her words as their truth.
Collective harmony seems worlds away,
As well the education of the youth.
Perhaps the groundless barriers raised by those
Few Greenbelt dwellers can be understood
For they live a comfortable life and change
Would be anathema, a disturbance to their wood.
Yet one knows that change is bound to come
For Auroville is indeed the Spirit's home.

January 4, 2022

The Unfading Ray

What shall I of Heaven's grace attain
Who have unconsciously walked through the years,
Sang in joy of life and known life's pain
And wept a river of my rainfall tears,
At beauty I have lost and my spirit's mate,
Defacement of this earth whom I so love,
The sorrow for this world does not abate
And the challenged ways in which we humans move.
No promise do I wish of supernal joy,
Earth is my home despite disharmony
I feel I am nothing but an outworn toy
Of forces that would control our destiny.
But there is more than hope, there is the Path
Hewn by the Avatars who with us stay
The falsehood and its overpowering wrath
Bringing to us the Truth, the unfading Ray.

March 6, 2022

The Warring Tribes

How shall the warring tribes of ego men
Bridge the gap between the false and true
Have humans not tried to rise again and again
Seeking the way of Truth known to the few,

And failing, falling back upon one's pride,
One's hurt, and painful retribution seek.
But truly there is no place for men to hide,
Neither cowering to the strong or attacking the meek

In games where power and lust control and guide
The soul into the darkness where all is lost
And meet with those who would the Truth deride,
The soul sink down and in the darkness tossed

Only to repent in lives to come,
Scenarios of ultimate defeat,
Forgotten the sacred plane where is our home
And the Force Divine waiting our souls to meet.

January 1, 2022

The Work of Transformation

In the alleyways and cul-de-sacs of life
Where one is led and often goes astray
In the unpleasant fields of daily strife
We often lose the knowledge of the Way.
The path is challenging and strewn with stones
Of sharpness injuring our way towards the goal:
No prayer, no aspiration of the mind atones
For errors the body visits on the soul.
A jumble of fragments humans seem to be
For residing within is a hostile force at work.
We seem estranged from the divinity
And move as automatons who start and jerk
At every seeming opportunity.
When shall we wake and know ourselves within
And the work of transformation at last begin?

March 6, 2022

The World is Suffering

The world is suffering and deep in pain
And the disharmony of man has grown
To such a degree that earth must bear the strain
Of the opposition's plan to gain
Control by subterfuge and power lust,
Reduce the population by degrees
To win at any cost and gain the trust
Of the unknowing millions whom they will please
Until the moment when they annihilate
The masses and inject sterility
In their malignant effort to create
Nations of slaves to bow in humility
To the Lords of all the hemispheres
Who rule by violence inducing fears
Of retribution if they do not obey
And those of stouter will whom they aim to slay.

February 22, 2022

The World Made New

I feel this world aflame with disharmony,
The attempt of evil forces to retain control.
There seems on earth a growing disparity
And the bitterness of soul contesting soul.

This often painful divergence on the way
To an evolutionary leap
A masque of deceit appears the unruly play
Of entities who would the falsehood keep,

Barring out the Light to keep the old
Consciousness intact and evil rule
This sacred life; the spirit's flame grown cold
Humanity become the Terror's tool.

But those who have come know the truth behind
Creation that all are destined here or there
The glorious epiphany to find
The world made new by the avataric pair.

February 4, 2022

The World Remake

There is nought here but leads us to the grave
Or worse, a hungering unfulfilled.
What greater loss than if the soul awake
To darkness in the pits and disbelief
Having grown accustomed to the light.
O pilgrim spirit refuse the ego-road
Well-travelled, trod by countless erring feet,
But on a lonely height stand unafraid
For one who waits within thee is the guide.
His hand shall stay the hordes at evil's call,
His strength thy strength to face the foe and win
From death the body's immortality,
A compass ever fixed upon the truth,
A mind enabled that sees the guise of sin,
The heart become a universal heart
To hold the suffering world in its embrace
And know beyond all doubt the love that saves,
An alchemy change sorrow's songs to bliss
That man may forge the future of his fate,
This world remake once more to God's design.

This World Must Change

Once again this painful memory
As I listen to a haunting choral work
'O Sacrum Convivium' sweetly intoned.
Over and over again these harmonies
Resound in me yet only sadness reigns
And the sorrow of the world on me descends.
I pass a paraplegic in a chair
Pushed resolutely by a wizened hag
And in the chair it is myself I see,
Head immense, lolling, the twisted form,
Distorted face, passionless and mute.
The tears unbidden flow – this world must change
And grief give room for joy to take its stand.
So shall the Overman transitioning
Be born into this world of human clay,
The predecessor of the superman
When light shall fill the earth and sorrow cease
And truth come down to occupy life's throne.

Thy Children Call

No longer hide behind the veil
O Lord, the world cries out to thee,
Though we struggle and though we fail
We heed thy call, "Remember me".

From the chrysalis of ignorance
Emerge thou say'st and know and be,
But in this world of fate and change
The night seems an eternity

And day but little time to grow
Into the image we adore,
O come sweet Mother and teach us how
To love and serve Thee evermore.

To Conquer Evil's Night

I have been witness to this world's decay,
Or so it seems when we are led astray
By leaders who profess the truth yet lie
Hoping that our high ideals might die
The ignominious death of human tools,
Considered nothing more than blinded fools
Who live and die never having known
The Light and in the densest darkness grown
Slaves of the few who seek a stranglehold
Of wealth and power in their noxious fold,
Empowered to destroy and to create
A hegemony, a philosophy of hate
And ultimate control of human beings:
But they will surely lose and all deceivings
Vanish when the Truth Supreme is here.
World of men I ask you not to fear
But hold within your souls the power of Light
And you will live to conquer evil's night.

March 6, 2022

Truth and Unity

It is the eve and all is still
When we celebrate the coming down
Of the Mother who all the worlds doth fill,
And we, have we towards Her grown
Or is this world still misery,
A driven race who hug their kind
Who cherish animosity
Believing humanity is blind.
How falsehood rampant on earth has grown
Sowing seeds of disharmony
But there are some who destined know
The way to Truth and Unity.

February 20, 2022

Truth its Way Will Find

They are dying now of the vaccines,
Athletes in the prime of life.
We are witnessing horrendous scenes
Of illegitimacy and strife
Attenuated by falsehood's ploys
Attacking senior citizens
And sparing not young girls and boys,
These dark unruly denizens.
When will evil's role be done
Attacking all the good of earth?
It seems that darkness now has won
Of its influence there is no dearth,
But there are some God-aligned
Who know that Truth its way will find.

February 4, 2022

Truth the Justicer

Now is the flower of the New Year full
And dawns a brighter year in youthful hearts,
Though winters we must face we still shall keep
The harvest of our love when day departs.
For who can see what joy the morrow brings
Or fathom tragedy and loss and fate,
But walk our metred walk apace our dreams
And hope that human good shall outlast hate.

Sleep then you souls, you children of the earth
And let your waking hours fill with song
For what shall be is written in His book
And Truth shall be the justicer of wrong.

Turning of an Age

We stand now at the turning of an age
Where evil minions hoping to impress
A unity of men as in a cage
Where none dispute their wisdom and holiness.

Perhaps it presages the iron age
At end and soon the world will turn to gold.
These are the words of the Avatar and sage
But we must fight against the sterile cold

Of minds that hope to master life and rule
The populace and prod them to remove
All doubt or else become the ages fool
Living out life in an eternal groove

Where Titan beings plan all to deceive
And take from man the Truth that he must live.

January 26, 2022

Upon the Earth

How does one choose when wrong appears to be right?
The entities of darkness shield their plans
And through the media engage the fight
To demonize the world evil demands.

Protectors of their right, the demon horde,
The children of the Light must battle through,
Most powerful for them the divinised word
Against the plethora of evil and the few

But powerful alliances they face
Upon this earth this cherished honored soil
Who bears with dignity the world's disgrace,
Alive, aware and conscious in its toil,

Marking out the vision of a race
Imbued with beauty, love and saving grace.

January 20, 2022

We Have Had Enough

"Where now the swarthy ferryman asks the crowd,
Do you wish to venture toward the distant shore?,
And hears in return a babble of voices loud
Reply, "Row us there and let us moor

On safer land where we may rest secure.
On dangerous fronts we certainly would not stray,
Safe islands call us for a lovely tour
Filled with joy and beauty and the array

Of fruits and juices wonderful to drink
And nighttime pleasures beneath the glowing moon
Where mind intoxicated needs not to think,
We would not dare the heaving main so soon.

But let us rest and lie with pleasure awhile
We have had enough of evil, falsehood and guile."

January 19, 2022

We Try

"We try" they say and then desire comes
And all that once was gained now is lost;
Difficult the path for those who stray
Unaware of the struggling spirit's cost.

For centuries there has been little growth
And man remains a little higher than
The animal, but barely so it seems
Thwarting or delaying Divinity's plan

To rise above the ego and be free,
Surrendered in joy to peace and the spirit's gain
To heights that physical mind can never know,
Above all human illnesses and pain.

A time will come when a few will take the leap
And the sacred promise of the Lord will keep.

January 19, 2022

What We Need Most

I hear the hammers on the busy street
Pounding out another day of toil
I see the motorcycles streaming past
All India seems at once to spoil

Her earth with urine and disposable waste.
Will she one day recover beauty as before
When temples rose and gods and angels heard
The chant of OM so powerful and pure

And prayer most genuine on her soil reigned.
What we need most is to surrender all
The things called wealth we cherish and adore
The gold, the baubles accumulated, or fall

Prey to forces intent to stay the Word,
The silent voice we once in stillness heard.

January 2, 2022

When Illness Comes

In days of illness the mind turns round and round
No inspiration able to pierce through
The numbing haze and the dark surround
As body strives its stability to renew.

But there are forces inimical to health
And minor gods who relish drama and play
Upon the consciousness and the wealth
Of silence and the peace for which we pray.

Recovery is slow when fever comes,
There is at times unsettling of soul
And pain in all its fury bites and numbs
The forward-looking spirit and takes its toll.

One must bear attacks of forces negative,
Hold close to Truth and always choose to live.

January 19, 2022

International Publications

Auroville Architecture
by Franz Fassbender

Auroville Form Style and Design
by Franz Fassbender

Landscapes and Gardens of Auroville
by Franz Fassbender

Inauguration of Auroville
by Franz Fassbender

Auroville in a Nutshell
by Tim Wrey

Death doesn't exist
The Mother on Death, Sri Aurobindo on Rebirth
Compiled by Franz Fassbender

Divine Love
Compiled by Franz Fassbender

Five Dream
by Sri Aurobindo

A Vision
Compiled by Franz Fassbender

Passage to More than India
by Dick Batstone

The Mother on Japan
Compiled by Franz Fassbender

Children of Change: A Spiritual Pilgrimage
by Amrit (Howard Shoji Iriyama)

Memories of Auroville - told by early Aurovilians
by Janet Feran

The Journeying Years
by Dianna Bowler

Auroville Reflected
by Bindu Mohanty

Finding the Psychic Being
by Loretta Shartsis

The Teachings of Flowers
The Life and Work of the Mother of the Sri Aurobindo Ashram
by Loretta Shartsis

The Supramental Transformation
by Loretta Shartsis

The Mother's Yoga - 1956-1973 (English & French)
Vol. 1, 1956-1967 & Vol. 2, 1968-1973
by Loretta Shartsis

Antithesis of Yoga
by Jocelyn Janaka

Bougainvilleas PROTECTION
by Narad (Richard Eggenberger), Nilisha Mehta

Crossroad The New Humanity
by Paulette Hadnagy

Die Praxis Des Integralen Yoga
by M. P. Pandit

The Way of the Sunlit Path
by William Sullivan

Wildlife great and small of India's Coromandel
by Tim Wrey

A New Education With A Soul
by Marguerite Smithwhite

Featured Titles

Divine Love

The texts presented in this book are selected from the Mother and Sri Aurobindo.
"Awakened to the meaning of my heart. That to feel love and oneness is to live. And this the magic of our golden change, is all the truth I know or seek, O sage."

Sri Aurobindo, Savitri, Book XII, Epilog

A Vision by the Mother

On 28th May 1958, the Mother recounted a vision she once had of a wonderful Being of Love and Consciousness, emanated from the Supreme Origin and projected directly into the Inconscient so that the creation would gradually awaken to the Supramental Consciousness. The Mother's account of this vision was brought out a first time in November 1906, in the Revue Cosmique, a monthly review published in Paris.

A Dream – Aims and Ideals of Auroville
the Mother on Auroville

50 years of Auroville from 28.02.1968 - 28.02.2018
Today, information about Auroville is abundant. Many people try to make meaning out of Auroville – about its conception, to what direction should we grow towards, and, what are we doing here?

But what was Mother's original Dream and what was her Vision for Auroville back then?

Matrimandir Talks by the Mother

This book presents most of Mother's Matrimandir talks, including how she conceived the idea for this special concentration and meditation building in Auroville.

Memories of Auroville - Told by early Aurovilians

Memories of Auroville is a book about the very early days of Auroville based on interviews made in 1997 with Aurovilians who lived here between 1968 and 1973. The interviews presented in this book are part of a history program for newcomers that I had created with my friend, Philip Melville in 1997. The plan was to divide Auroville's history into different eras and then interview Aurovilians according to their area of knowledge.
Our first section would cover the years from 1968 till 1973 when the Mother was still in her physical body.

The Way of the Sunlit Path

May The Way of the Sunlit Path be a convenient guide for activating this ancient truth as a support for a Conscious Evolution.
May it illumine the transformation offered to us in the Integral Yoga.

A Dream Takes Shape (in English, French, Hindi)

A comprehensive brochure on the international township of Auroville in, ranging from its Charter and "Why Auroville?" to the plan of the township, the central Matrimandir, the national pavilions and residences, to working groups, the economy, making visits, how to join, its relationship to the Sri Aurobindo Ashram, and its key role in the future of the world. This brochure endeavours to highlight how The Mother envisioned Auroville from its inception, some of the major achievements realised over the years, and some of the difficulties currently faced in implementing the guidelines which she gave.

Mother on Japan

I had everything to learn in Japan. For four years, from an artistic point of view, I lived from wonder to wonder. And everything in this city, in this country, from beginning to end, gives you the impression of impermanence, of the unexpected, the exceptional... ...everything in this city, in this country, from beginning to end, gives you the impression of impermanence, of the unexpected, the exceptional. You always come to things you did not expect; you want to find them again and they are lost – they have made something else which is equally charming.

Auroville Reflected

On 28 February 1968, on an impoverished plateau on the Coromandel Coast of South India, about 4,000 people from around the world gathered for a most unusual inauguration. Handfuls of soil from the countries of the world were mixed together as a symbol of human unity. Why did Indira Gandhi, the erstwhile Prime Minister of India, support this development for "a city the earth needs?" Why did UNESCO endorse this project? Why does the Dalai Lama continue to be involved in the project? What led anthropologist Margaret Mead to insist that records must be kept of its progress? Why did both historian William Irwin Thompson and United Nations representative Robert Muller note that this social experiment may be a breakthrough for humanity even as critics commented, "it is an impossible dream"?

A House For the Third Millennium
Essays on Matrimandir

Nightwatch at the Matrimandir...
A cosmic spectacle; the black expanse above, the big black crater of Matrimandir's excavation carved deep into the soil. The four pillars - two of which are completed and the other two nearing completion - are four huge ships coming together from the four corners of the earth to meet at this pro propitious spot...

Passage to More than India

This book is a voyage of discovery. In 1959 the author, Dick Batstone, a classically educated bookseller in England, with a Christian background, comes across a life of the great Indian polymath Sri Aurobindo, though a series of apparently fortuitous circumstances. A meeting in Durham, England, leads him to a determination to get to the Sri Aurobindo Ashram in Pondicherry, a former French territory south of Madras.

www.ingramcontent.com/pod-product-compliance
Lightning Source LLC
LaVergne TN
LVHW021304080526
838199LV00090B/6006